PUPPY

HOW TO USE THIS BOOK

Read the captions in the eight-page booklet and, using the labels beside each sticker, choose the image that best fits in the space available.

•

Don't forget that your stickers can be stuck down and peeled off again. If you are careful, you can use your puppy stickers more than once.

•

You can also use the stickers to decorate your own books, or for project work at school.

LONDON, NEW YORK, MUNICH,
MELBOURNE, DELHI

First American Edition, 1996
This Edition, 2005

10 11 12 13 10 9 8 7

Published in the United States by DK Publishing, Inc.,
375 Hudson Street, New York, New York, 10014

Copyright © 1996, 2005, Dorling Kindersley Limited

ISBN-13: 978-0-7566-1458-4

Reproduced by Media Development and Printing Ltd, UK
Printed and bound by L. Rex, China

Discover more at
www.dk.com

Playing and learning

 Puppies are constantly alert and need lots of exercise. Playing games not only provides the necessary exercise, it helps a puppy bond with its litter or its owner, and stops it from becoming destructive. A puppy also learns about balance and coordination through play, and builds strength. Puppies have a natural desire to search and chase, and will play energetically.

Scent clues
Once a puppy's senses have developed, it becomes very curious and starts to explore its surroundings. Early on, puppies begin to learn about the smells other animals leave behind.

Enough is enough
Energetic play is part of every healthy young dog's life. But sleep is also important, and these puppies have worn themselves out. Dogs often sleep with their backs against something comforting or protective.

Getting around
Newborn puppies use scent and heat to find their mothers. At three weeks, other senses take over. The touch sensors on their paws have developed, too, which helps them build independence.

Contact sport
Making contact with other puppies is vital to a young dog's development. Dogs use their body movements to communicate, and puppies must learn to understand the signals.

From play to work
Toys don't just keep puppies happy! As this dog chews on its bone, it is strengthening its neck and jaw muscles.

Bowing down
This is the position that dogs use to show they are not being aggressive, but rather that they are friendly. Puppies often use this position when they play, asking other dogs to join in their games.

Balancing act
When a puppy finds a new toy, it will touch and pat it before tasting it. This means standing on one front paw, which helps develop balance.

Attention seeking
Puppies are natural pack animals, and therefore need attention and company. Being held by its owner makes this puppy feel safe and happy, and being stroked relaxes it.

Fearless fighters
When they are young, puppies don't understand fear. They will play-fight with other puppies regardless of their size and strength. At about eight weeks they develop more cautious behavior, and become careful when play-fighting.

Friend or foe
When a puppy first meets an older dog, it learns about social behavior. If the dog is friendly, the puppy learns that they can meet and play without any need to fight.

Playing safe
It is important that puppies have their own toys to play with, otherwise they will help themselves to yours. Plastic or rubber toys are safer than sticks and stones.

Leader of the pack
Once a puppy has left its mother, it looks to its owner for help and guidance. A puppy will rely on its owner to play with it and provide food and exercise.

Good enough to eat
Having sniffed and tasted this new toy, this puppy is bowing to it, showing that it is excited and ready to play.

Dog-napping
Although puppies need more sleep, all dogs doze throughout the day. Yawning usually means they are about to settle down, and shows they are totally relaxed.

Biting back
It is natural pack behavior for puppies to bite when they play. They learn about their own strength and how other puppies will react to them if they are aggressive.

Licked into shape
Grooming is one of the things that puppies learn from their mother. While they are young, they often copy her behavior and practice grooming each other. It can be a sign of friendship.

Keeping guard
Puppies naturally guard and protect their toys, food, and even their owners. They may show aggression if they feel threatened by other puppies.

Various breeds

 All domestic puppies are related to the Gray Wolf. There are more than 400 types of pedigree dogs, most of which have developed from working dogs. Each breed has certain characteristics such as better sight, smell, or strength, that make it different from other dogs. Most puppies are the same size when they are young, regardless of their breed, and they can look very different from their parents.

Black beauty
The Labrador Retriever is one of the most intelligent, loyal, and responsive breeds. Labradors are very good with children, and make reliable family pets.

Fiery redhead
The Spaniel developed in Britain as a hunting dog. Spaniels that are one color can have a more aggressive nature than multicolored varieties.

Father and son
The Caucasian Sheepdog was developed to herd and protect sheep on the harsh mountains of the former USSR. It is tall and strong, and has a thick, warm coat.

Mistaken identity
The Great Dane was developed in Germany, where it was used to guard castles. The puppies are born with adult-sized feet, and look clumsy until their bodies have caught up in size.

Bundle of gold
This Golden Retriever puppy is only one week old. It looks very different from its mother now, but within six months its coat and markings will be fully developed.

Puppy fat
Shar Pei puppies are covered in big folds of skin that remain visible when they are adult. It makes them look sad, but in fact Shar Peis are calm, gentle, and independent dogs.

Tiny terror
Jack Russell Terriers are small, lively puppies, growing only about 14 in (35 cm) tall. They have either brown, black, or orange markings.

Giant eaters
Great Dane puppies are friendly, tolerant, and gentle. They make excellent family pets – except for the huge food bills!

PUPPY PLAY

Golden Retrievers
tussling

A perfect pedigree litter
on the lookout

Six-week-old puppies,
tired after a run

Four-week-old Great
Dane puppies nuzzling

Curious puppies using
their noses

Learning to play

An older puppy
greeting a friend

Play-fighting Labradors

Skye Terrier puppies
with their tiny mom

A sleepy family
resting after a busy day

Making an
unusual
friend

Getting a
special treat

This Collie is
ready for a walk

Crossbreed puppies ready to explore

A Spaniel and a Retriever
sharing a meal

PUPPY SHOW

A thick-coated
black puppy

A silky
red Spaniel

A tall Irish
Wolfhound and
his tiny pup

An Australian
Cattle Dog

A well-traveled
puppy

A Caucasian Sheepdog
puppy with its father

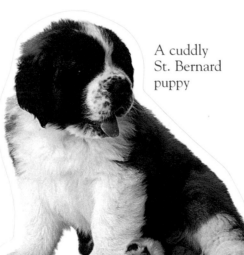

Old English Sheepdogs

A West Highland
White Terrier

A cuddly
St. Bernard
puppy

A playful crossbreed puppy

A sleepy Spaniel

Settling into a
new home

A well-groomed
Yorkshire Terrier
puppy

Golden Retriever
playmates

Australian Cattle
Dog puppies

PUPPY SHOW

A curious
Spaniel puppy

Discovering
new toys

Retrievers with
short puppy hair

This Labrador is
learning to pounce

Young puppies
nursing

A proud mom with
her pedigree litter

Teething with a
plastic bone

A Golden Retriever puppy

A two-week-old
wrinkly pup

Tracking a scent

Wrinkly Great
Dane puppies
wrestling

A Shar Pei puppy

A Great Dane
puppy

A Spaniel
puppy

A colorful Jack
Russell

PUPPY LIFE

A healthy Terrier

Keeping your puppy clean

Italian Greyhound puppies staying near mom

Thick-coated mountain puppies curling up to stay warm

A Canary puppy pestering dad

Older puppies still trying to nurse

A Terrier proudly wearing its new collar

A Retriever puppy enjoying his meal

A Spaniel pleading for food

Friendly Australian Cattle Dog puppies taking a break

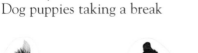

An exhausted young puppy yawning

Getting lots of attention

This long-legged puppy will fill out

A new partnership

The best of friends

Mixed bunch
A crossbreed puppy has a mother and father from different breeds, and can have characteristics of both. There are many more crossbreeds than pedigree breeds.

Powerful pair
This Canary puppy is sitting with its powerful father. Like Shar Peis, Canary dogs have loose, wrinkly skin. The puppies are determined and strong.

Mountain climbers
These stocky puppies are strong mountain dogs. The black one is a Bernese Mountain Dog. In the past, Bernese were used in Switzerland to pull carts carrying market produce.

Scots guard
West Highland White Terrier puppies are not much smaller than their tiny parents. They are affectionate and lively puppies. Surprisingly, "Westies" also make excellent guard dogs.

Pale imitation
This small, fluffy puppy will grow into a strong Australian Cattle Dog. Its coat will get much darker, and its markings more obvious. The white coloring comes from Dalmatian blood in its ancestry.

Unique pet
This puppy is a crossbreed. Some people believe crossbreed puppies make friendlier household pets than pedigree puppies.

Veiled Terrier
These Skye Terriers have beautiful, long coats that need regular grooming to stay clean and shiny. The hair on their heads is shorter, and when the puppies get older, it will form a curtain over their eyes.

Sleepy Spaniel
Cocker Spaniels are active and playful puppies. They show their excitement by wagging their tails furiously. After racing around, this puppy is ready for a nap.

Family favorite
The color of the Golden Retriever's coat is one reason why it is among the most popular of dogs. It is an easy puppy to train, and enjoys family life as long as it gets plenty of exercise.

Puppy care

Puppies have many of the same instincts as humans. They enjoy friendship, and prefer living either with their litter or as a member of a human family. A puppy will be old enough to leave its litter at about nine weeks. It is important to train a puppy, while still young, so that it will fit happily into its home.

Traveling light
Puppies often have to visit the vet during the first few months of their lives, and a safe, secure carrier box provides the easiest way to get them there.

Brotherly love
It is very important that puppies develop friendships while they are young so that they learn to communicate. It will help them grow into friendly, confident dogs.

Dry cleaning
Giving this puppy a regular brush will keep its coat shiny and clean. It also gives its owner a chance to check for health problems and hair loss.

Three's a crowd
At five weeks old, these puppies are no longer entirely dependent on their mother. All their senses are fully developed. Soon they won't even need each other and will happily explore alone.

Body language
You can tell that this puppy is happy because its tail is raised and wagging and its ears are in a relaxed position. Puppies have very clear signs to tell us how they are feeling.

Collar practice
Puppies should start to wear a collar when they are about six weeks old, but only for a short time each day until they are used to it. The size of the collar must be checked regularly as the puppy grows.

Comfort food
These six-week-old puppies don't need their mother's milk anymore. She allows them to nurse though, because it is comforting for both her and her growing litter.

A helping hand
When a puppy leaves its mother, its owner becomes its mother instead. Grooming a puppy helps develop this bond, and keeps it clean at the same time.

A dog's life
Young puppies spend most of their time either feeding or sleeping. In between they will become very excited in short bursts. This is normal in a healthy puppy.

Bedtime
Puppies are very sociable and enjoy being with people even when they're tired, so the best place for a puppy's bed is in a busy part of its house. It is best not to buy a hard bed for a puppy until it has stopped teething.

Dining alone
As a puppy gets older, its natural instinct is to protect its food from other dogs, just as it would in the wild. It may growl if anyone gets too close, so it is best to let a young dog eat alone.

Special treats
Puppies are comforted by attention and touch. This young puppy is happy to get a treat from its new owner, and they will become friends through this contact.

Helpless bundles
As soon as all her puppies are born, a mother cleans them and lets them feed. Puppies are almost totally helpless without their mother when first born.

All grown up
Puppies are all born roughly the same size regardless of how big they may grow. When choosing a dog, it is important to keep its adult size and need for exercise in mind.

Taking a walk
As a puppy grows, it needs more space to exercise. While they are still young, puppies should be taught to walk on a leash without getting nervous or over-excited.

Mother's pride
This mother is relaxing with her young litter. Her puppies constantly want to feed, and, while they are small, it is a pleasurable activity for her.

Tricks of the trade
These puppies are looking up pleadingly, hoping for food or attention. They learned to do this with their mothers, and now show the same behavior with their owner.

Puppies in training

Not all puppies become simply pets. Some puppies are chosen to be trained for work as adults. They may become farm dogs, racing dogs, or hunting dogs for instance. Puppies are chosen for these jobs because of certain qualities in their breed, such as strength, speed, or responsiveness.

Sheep's clothing
The Old English Sheepdog was bred to herd sheep. Its coat helped it hide among the sheep to surprise hungry, prowling wolves.

Worth their weight in gold
Golden Retriever puppies are often chosen to be guide dogs for blind owners. They are easy to train and make excellent companions.

Versatile puppies
Labrador puppies are used for many different types of work, including hunting. Originally from Canada, they used to help fishermen drag their nets ashore.

Australian Cattle Dog
Originally used to herd cattle in Australia, these puppies have thick coats, strong backs, and muscular legs. They are well behaved and hard workers.

Gentle gun dog
The Spaniel has a long, wide nose for smelling, and a gentle, delicate bite, making it the ideal puppy for tracking and retrieving game.

Friendly giant
This strong St. Bernard puppy was originally bred to search for and rescue people lost on mountains in Switzerland.

A little terrier
The Yorkshire Terrier was bred by miners to hunt for rats in mine pits. The puppies are playful and intelligent.

Elegant companion
Italian Greyhounds were historically kept as ladies' companions because they are quiet and friendly. Larger Greyhounds are used as racing dogs.